ENDORSEMENT

THE FAITHFULNESS OF GOD, OUTSIDE OF THE BOX:

> Pastor Lucas knows how to get *Out of the Box*. He is bold in following instructions from the Holy Spirit. His life and book are testimonies of how God rewards radical obedience. This book has some great illustrations on getting *Out of the Box*. It will encourage you to step out for Jesus.

> Joy Gartman, author

The Faithfulness of God outside of the box

The Faithfulness of God outside of the Box is a book which pertains how God shows His love, grace and faithfulness to each one that avails himself for the Lord. In this book God expounds the importance of obedience and humility, that as we obey Gods instruction or unction you will see his power and greatness manifest in a way that you will be amazed! God's faithfulness cannot be compared to anything that a man can imagined or think about.

Awesome and amazing things you will see in this book that you will desire to be an instrument of God for His goodness, experiencing His presence and mighty power, I indeed recommend this book to be a must read for all ages to experience and see Gods faithfulness. God is not a respecter of person. He shows His grace to everyone that avails himself for Him. He is the all- powerful and a limitless God that could not be put in a box.

"The Faithfulness of God"

If you are tired of today's powerless traditional experiences seen in most churches, this is the book to read. If you hunger for the supernatural Biblical experiences in your life, this is the book to read. This book gives the Body of Christ examples of what will happen to us, for us, and through us when we step out of the box and allow God to have His way.

Pastor Alan Myrick

T0146913

THE
FAITHFULNESS
OF GOD
OUTSIDE
THE BOX

JOHN H LUCAS JR.

ISBN: 978-1-4907-0506-4 (sc)
ISBN: 978-1-4907-0505-7 (e)

Trafford rev. 06/27/2013

 www.trafford.com

North America & international
toll-free: 1 888 232 4444 (USA & Canada)
phone: 250 383 6864 ♦ fax: 812 355 4082

ACKNOWLEDGEMENT

I must thank God for downloading this work for his glory and for all the prophetic words that gave me the grace to stay with it until completion.

I want to acknowledge my wife who is my best friend for her patience and wisdom in allowing me to leave home to write this book during one to most important times in our year and that was Thanksgiving 2012 for this I'm especially grateful to her, this book was a long process for me and with my wife's love and mercy we have finished the process. I would also like to thank the Gloryland Revival Center family for putting up with me during this awesome task, also allowing me time away in more ways than one, thank you. I Also would like to thank our spiritual daughter Merian Fernandez in Hong Kong who gave her all in writing up the testimonies from services in our outpouring Conference in Jesus The True Redeemer Church in Hong Kong, thank you.

Contents

Introduction

The faithfulness of God is something that you have to experience, not read about in your lives, and when I was young, I knew that God was real and there were things I would not do and things that I wouldn't say because I was always aware of his presence. God spoke to me when I was drowning, and from that day until now, his presence is what I desire. Psalm 42:1-5, is one of my favorite scriptures because, as Moses said, "Lord, if I have found favor in your sight, show me your Glory. This is what I desire more than anything." The reason I'm writing this book is to that degree, I want to see the body of Christ functioning as I see in the book of Acts.

When I was in this certain denomination twenty years ago, I read the book of Acts and something was different, and so I began to seek the Lord more and more to answer this burning in my heart for more. In that church, I didn't see what I was seeing in the

Bible, and it seemed like only a few were really hungry for more.

This led me on a path of hunger that can only be quenched by God's presence, but I found out that most of us have put him into this box of our programmed thinking, which depicts God as one who can only work through certain people who have these titles and so on. But the Bible tells me that these signs shall follow them that believe, Mark 16:16-18, not just pastors, apostles, prophets, teachers, and evangelists but he that believes, Romans 12:1-2, is one of the keys that we need to work the works of Christ while it is day. We need to change the way we think. We need the true Gospel, and this is that God's Son died for the sins of the world, and he gave us the power and authority to move as he moved and do as he did.

One of the things I must say is it's not so we can get the glory but the people who need to be set free from diseases and sicknesses, demonic influences, and every negative thing that has happened to them. And when we do it his way, only God gets the glory.

In closing, Jesus said that the works that he did, we can do greater. Draw near to God, and he will draw near to you. Seek and you shall find. Knock and it shall be opened to you. Changed thinking equals different results.

My prayer is that when you read this book, you will be changed forever and begin to let fear go and wrong thinking and realize God has chosen you also.

God bless you more and more.

John H. Lucas Jr.

Chapter One

OBEDIENCE

I was not a slave in the sense of slavery, but being born during the time, we had colored water fountains and toilets in public places. It shaped my way of looking at everything, including God's Word. People were always saying we couldn't learn or do anything. That puts you in a box, but you don't realize it. You just think it's normal.

Being born in North Carolina without a father who passed when I was two years old was something that caused rebellion in my life at a young age. But it was soon driven out of me by a mother who was strong and very persuasive when she spoke. She was not abusive, but she was very direct. I had three sisters, and I'm the only boy, so I did get some special treatment at times, as well as discipline. We went to church all the time as young people because we were made to go. I must note that my mother was

5'10" tall and she was 180 pounds, not fat. But to us, she was a giant. I'm 6'4" tall and my dad was 6'2", so I'm naturally tall. As we went to church, we were very active in church. I truly enjoyed it because some of my friends went to the same AME Church in my hometown. Something happened to me when it came to discipline. When I would get in trouble, my mother would tell me to sit in a chair until she returned from shopping. I wouldn't move until she returned from shopping or going downtown or anywhere because I had the fear of Susie Lucas on me. I believe this was a precursor to God beginning my school of obedience. I remember once trying to read Watchman Nee's book *Spriritual Authority*. It was so deep, I would read a couple of pages and set it down for a month because I couldn't read it because it speaks on obedience to another level.

While attending Bible college, I discovered some powerful things. One was when we did a timeline on our life from birth to the present. I saw the Hand of God on my life like I had not seen anytime before, and I then realized that God had me in his hands way before I was born.

Eph. 1:4 according as he hath chosen us in him before the foundation of the world, that we should be holy and without blame before him in love:

Eph. 1:5 having predestinated us unto the adoption of children by Jesus Christ to himself, according to the good pleasure of his will, God chose us before the foundation of the world.

He knew you and me. That was a major revelation to who I am and who I am for me. As I was being taught obedience, I went through some awesome experiences. Going into a Sears and Roebuck Store one day, I had to go to the bathroom, and as I was finishing my business, I noticed that the bathroom was filthy and I complained about it. The Lord said "clean it up," and pride tried to overtake me because I thought "what if someone I know comes in here and sees me cleaning this bathroom?" But I was unaware of what the Lord was doing in me (I'm speaking not like I have arrived).

I would go to the bathroom at the service stations, and the Lord would say "clean it up." Part of the lesson was not complaining about anything. It didn't stop there; more training was needed.

One day, the Lord said to me that I have offended three people that I worked with. He said "go to them and get it straight." It took me two weeks to obey this one, but when I did, we cried, and they forgave me because God had already prepared their hearts. That was a turning point where I began to understand our God is so awesome and faithful to his word. I saw that it's better to obey than sacrifice.

1 Samuel 15:22 states, "and Samuel said, hath the Lord *as great* delight in burnt offerings and sacrifices, as in obeying the voice of the Lord? Behold, to obey *is* better than sacrifice, *and* to hearken than the fat of rams."

One of the keys to obeying is hearing the voice of God, and before you can hear, you must know his voice. In other words, we must be intimate with his voice:

> John_10:3 to him the porter openeth; and the sheep hear his voice: and he calleth his own sheep by name, and leadeth them out.

> John_10:4 and when he putteth forth his own sheep, he goeth before them, and the sheep follow him: for they know his voice.

> John_10:5 and a stranger will they not follow, but will flee from him: for they know not the voice of strangers.

We must recognize and be intimate, know, perceive, and understand his voice. It began with me when I was twelve years old, when I almost drowned in a ditch. Some friends and I were playing near a ditch, and they said "let's get in." So, being very proud and not wanting to appear afraid, I jumped in with everyone, and before I knew it, I was underwater and I couldn't swim. I jumped up three, four, and five times to get my head from under the water. I tried to climb out to no avail, and then I jumped some more and got really tired, and I knew at that time I was not going to make it. I was dying, and I just said within myself, "Lord, I'm ready." And for the first time in my life, I heard the voice (not an audible voice, but from within my spirit) that said, "Get out of the water." And to my amazement, I got out and went home, and my mother asked me what was wrong. I didn't say anything to her. I took a bath because the water was muddy, and I went to sleep in the middle of the day until the next morning.

I really didn't understand that at the time, but now I do. He has something for us to do, and we are predestined for that work wherein he has called you to do, and the enemy can't stop it. Only we can. If we faint not, we shall reap the harvest. Don't turn back.

Gal. 6:9 and let us not be weary in well doing: for in due season we shall reap, if we faint not.

Heb. 10:38 now the just shall live by faith: but if *any man* draw back, my soul shall have no pleasure in him.

Heb. 10:39 but we are not of them who draw back unto perdition; but of them that believe to the saving of the soul.

This is what the Lord wants in us is obedience, he wants out of our boxes so his true identity can be released into the earth, he wants to use you Jesus said the works that I do, greater shall you do because he went back to the Father

John 14:12 verily, verily, I say unto you, he that believeth on me, the works that I do shall he do also; and greater *works* than these shall he do; because I go unto my Father.

This does not mean the servant is greater than his master but that he wants you to display him in these works.

John 13:16 verily, verily, I say unto you, the servant is not greater than his lord; neither he that is sent greater than he that sent him.

Next step: humility.

Chapter Two

Humility

The Bible expresses this subject very seriously in the fact that Jesus, when he came in humility and meekness, was obedient and submissive to the will of the Father. So must we be if we are to be Christlike. Humility—the Bible says that we either humble ourselves, or we will be humbled.

> **Matt. 18:3** and said, verily I say unto you, except ye be converted, and become as little children, ye shall not enter into the kingdom of heaven.

> Matt. 18:4 whosoever therefore shall humble himself as this little child, the same is greatest in the kingdom of heaven.

The context of these verses is talking about being childlike (as a child). They may get angry when they are playing with other children, but before you know it, they are playing like nothing ever went wrong. That's an example that came to me as I write because they are humble to the degree that they'd rather play than lose that friend, because it's about playing and having fun. But on the other hand, as adults, we want to humble ourselves so we can have fun or keep that lifelong friend.

Jesus said that he that exalts himself shall be abased.

Matt. 23:12 and whosoever shall exalt himself shall be abased; and he that shall humble himself shall be exalted.

The word "abased" in the Greek means to *depress*, figuratively to *humiliate* (in condition or heart), or to bring low, humble (self).

In other words, it's better to humble yourself.

How can God use someone who thinks he's better than God? We know of Lucifer and his fall. Isaiah 14:12 states, "How art thou fallen from heaven, o Lucifer, son of the morning! *How* art thou cut down to the ground, which didst weaken the nations!"

Pride keeps God in the box and you on the throne. That was Satan's mistake—trying to exalt himself above the most high God.

One day, my wife and I were cleaning out the flower bed to plant some fresh new ones, and I told her I would go to the gas station to get gas for the rototiller. As I was driving, I heard what seemed like many ambulances going near where I was going, and as I drove onto that street, the traffic had backed up because of a four-car accident. The street was so wide, I was able to drive on the side until I reached the service station, going around the accident.

But as I was driving into the station, the Lord said, "You're a minister. Go and tell the ambulance attendant and offer your assistance."

And I said, "I'm not going to do that."

And he repeated it again. "Go and offer your assistance."

I said OK, and I went to the paramedic and said, "I'm a minister. Can I help you?"

And she screamed and said to me, "You better get out of the way and get back on that sidewalk!"

And I immediately retaliated and said in a loud voice, "You could have said no."

As I walked away, dejected and hurt, the Lord said, "You got offended, didn't you?"

And I stood there and repented and realized I had pride that was hidden in myself that was only exposed because I thought I was all that and a bag of chips. During that time, I was praying, "Lord, show me myself."

Be careful what you pray for, but I thank God for exposing the things that would eventually destroy me or stop what the Lord was trying to accomplish in me.

Experience is the best teacher. I believe these lessons are there not to destroy you, but to prepare you for the greater works. Jeremiah 29:11 states, "I know the plans that I have for you, declares the Lord. They are plans for peace and not disaster, plans to give you a future filled with hope" (God's Word Version).

You must first be willing to humble yourself to receive the grace of God for ministry. I heard a powerful definition of grace from a pastor from Michigan while my wife and I were in the British Virgin Islands, Tortola, at a conference. He said that grace is the empowering presence of God enabling me to be who God called me to be and do the things he's called me to do—not just unmerited favor, but an enabling. The dictionary defines *enabling* as "conferring new legal powers or capacities, by removing a disability, to make able, give power, means, competence, ability to; to authorize." I will talk more about this later, God's grace.

Like obedience, grace can be misused or ignored. Hebrews 13:9 states: "Do not be carried about by different *and* varied and alien teachings; for it is good for the heart to be established *and* ennobled *and* strengthened by means of grace (God's favor and spiritual blessing) and not [to be devoted to] foods [rules of diet and ritualistic meals], which bring no [spiritual] benefit *or* profit to those who observe them" (AMP).

This is talking about the law or to be the box of performance, or if I do this God will do that it is finished says the Lord, also God's grace is not just vertical from God to man but horizontal from man to man which gives us the cross.

God wants to use you mightily for his glory. I believe we are entering into the greatest days of the church, or the kingdom of God (which are the same), and the kingdom of God is within us.

(Luke 17:21) they can't say, 'here it is!' or 'there it is!' you see, the kingdom of God is within you." (KJV)

We are the church, and the kingdom is in the church—us. Praise God. The Bible says the kingdom is not meat or drink but righteousness, peace, and joy in the Holy Ghost.

(Romans 14:17) for God's kingdom is not a matter of eating and drinking, but of the righteousness, peace, and joy which the Holy Spirit gives (Good News Bible).

It's not a matter of what you do but what Christ did. Is the box opened? Please let him out.

We must humble ourselves, this is the way of the kingdom, and Jesus humbled himself and died on an old rugged cross for you and me. God gives grace to the humble, but he resists the proud.

Chapter Three

Grace

We have already established that grace is not just unmerited favor, but an enabling—God's grace enabling me to be and do what he called me to be and do. My spiritual mother used to say God never made us "human doings," but "human beings." In other words, it's about being who God wants you to be or who he created you to be. You're not a mistake. You're not a last-minute thought. You were on his mind before the foundations of the world. Wow, that's glorious indeed. I was on his mind.

I'm a pastor/missionary, and when I first went on a mission trip to the Philippines, I noticed something different started happening in the services that I have never seen before. I didn't understand it, so I just enjoyed it but didn't know really what was happening. But I have always known that God called me with a holy calling and the confidence that comes after you have ministered a while, but this was not confidence but another anointing that would only come on me when I was overseas in the place God called me to on the mission field, and that's very important.

The reason being in the place God has chosen for you is the anointing is strongest when you are in his perfect will. Now remember, the calling of God is without repentance. **Romans 11:29** says, "For the gifts and the calling of God *are* without repentance."

This means God won't repent for the gifts he gave you no matter if you are in his perfect will or not. But we know it's better to be in his perfect will. So the Lord is ready to glorify himself through you when you are obedient to his will and purposes for your life.

I finally found out what this was that came over me, and I was invited to attend a conference in Santa Nella, California. And after that we were due for our 2006 trip with Apostle Angel Perez and the team.

The first day of the conference was incredible, and it got better every day afterward, but on the second day something happened that opened up some great understanding, and then I knew what was coming over me on mission trips. The speaker was Prophetess/ Mother Jean Krisle (Blasi). She spoke to me and said that when you go overseas, there's a grace that would come on you that you wished would never leave. What I'm talking about this grace enables you to do things that you would normally not be able to do. A supernatural power would come, and you could do as the book of Samuel says it. **2 Samuel 22:30** states that "for by thee I have run through a troop: by my God have I leaped over a wall." I believe Sid Roth says that we should live naturally supernaturally; the Holy Ghost gives us power to be and do everything God has equipped us to be and do.

With this grace, your faith is at another level. It supersedes your normal level of faith. You do and say things that you say afterward to yourself: Did I say that? Did I do that? But let me say this now. Remember this thing called *pride*. It will try to creep in if you don't remain in prayer. Before I understood what it was, I was getting angry with the people at home because I saw so many miracles there because of this grace, and at home, the people were setting down wanting to be entertained. The grace that comes on you there is a direct result of the hunger of the people you are ministering to. If there's no hunger they want, draw on the anointing in you. Oh, but you will never be the same when you experience this truly wonderful, glorious encounter—with this grace.

There's a price to pay for this grace. The Bible says that we must study to show ourselves approved, take a look at this commentary by Barnes: study to show thyself approved unto God—give diligence. 2 Peter 2:10, or make an effort so to discharge the duties of the ministerial office as to meet the divine approbation. The object of the ministry is not to please men. Such doctrines should be preached, and such plans formed, and such a manner of life pursued, as God will approve. To do this demands study or care—for there are many temptations to the opposite course; there are many things the tendency of which is to lead a minister to seek popular favor rather than the divine approval. If any man pleases God, it will be as the result of deliberate intention and a careful life.

I couldn't say it better. We have to study, and as we mature in Christ, the tendency to seek the popular favor of men dissipates, and we become vessels of honor, and the residue of the time spent studying (or I like to say being with the king) just flows out of you so freely. Remember, your faith increases—and now you are bolder, more direct, etc. I remember being in the mountain about three hours away from Cagayan de Oro in Mindanao, Philippines, and as we were in worship in the service, the Lord spoke to me. Andhe said "I will do what you say," and immediately, I changed the message to Matthew 8:16-17.

Matt. 8:16 When the even was come, they brought unto him many that were possessed with devils: and he cast out the spirits with *his* word, and healed all that were sick:

Matt. 8:17 That it might be fulfilled which was spoken by Esaias the prophet, saying, himself took our infirmities, and bare *our* sicknesses.

One thing that I must say here is that we must remember even though our hands are being laid on people it is to glorify the Lord.

You noticed the scripture in verse 16 talks about devils, and I can't tell you why I chose these verses but I believe God chose them for me, remember he's faithful outside of our boxes that we have set up or constructed, as I was finishing the message the Lord said call up the worship team and pray for them first. (I was using an interpreter.)

It was a large group so I didn't want to lay hands on all of them because I knew that I had more to do, so I waived my hand at them and they began to fall, but the man standing directly in front of me began to manifest like a vicious dog, growling and trying to leap at me but couldn't move from his spot the angle was in front of me for my protection, and the Lord said to me hit him in the stomach now three seconds later I hit him as hard as I could and he was completely delivered from every demon and filled with the Holy Ghost they baptized him in water, six months later he sent a message to me and said he was serving God and was totally free. During this meeting I ministered to many that were Demon possessed and sick, God healed them all, but one, the service was over they ask me to go to someone house and cast out a demon in a boy about 8 years old I prayed for an hour and I ask my interpreter to pray and I asked God why want this spirit come out, and he said that the fathers parents were into witchcraft and I ask the father to renounce it and he wouldn't so my assignment was up at that time I had no authority in that man's house without his permission, well that's another book. We are ever learning and growing in Christ.

This grace will transcend your thinking and the way you do things, do I understand it? No but knowing the voice of our God is very important in walking in this grace.

Remember our God is with you and will never leave you or forsake you even until the end of the ages.

One scripture to remember about the apostles, Acts 4:28 For to do whatsoever thy hand and thy counsel determined before to be done.

Acts 4:29 And now, Lord, behold their threatenings and grant unto thy servants, that with all boldness they may speak thy word,

Acts 4:30 By stretching forth thine hand to heal; and that signs and wonders may be done by the name of thy holy child Jesus.

Acts 4:31 And when they had prayed, the place was shaken where they were assembled together; and they were all filled with the Holy Ghost, and they spake the Word of God with boldness.

Acts 4:32 and the multitude of them believed were of one heart and of one soul: neither said any *of them* that ought of the things which he possessed was his own; but they had all things common.

Acts 4:33 and with great power gave the apostles witness of the resurrection of the Lord Jesus: and great grace was upon them all. (KJV)

They had favor, grace with God and man.

On our mission trips, we go to a place that many consider dangerous, and I believe that where sin abounds, grace does much more abound. You can operate in the most sinful areas, and this grace will abound over sin.

Abound means "to do, make or be more, that is, increase over sin." Amen

Chapter Four

Opening the Box

Jesus gave them this answer "Very truly I tell you, the son can do nothing by himself;[a] he can do only what he sees his father doing, because whatever the father does, the son also does" (John 5:19).

This passage of scripture came to life for me at a prayer retreat here in California, 2009, my wife and I went on a retreat together for the first time because usually we do it separately anyway it was great for both of us but the Lord spoke to me about this scripture in relationship to miracles and signs and wonders, even though I had seen some miracles I believe God wanted to expand my boarders, amen. He said that my son was always healing, delivering, casting out devils, and had never failed, and I took a look at it again. It opened up like a new baby. You can't take your eyes off it—the baby. I began to seek God in a different way in prayer, especially when I was going to minister. Any time we receive a new revelation, we have a tendency to release it too soon, and I did and didn't begin to understand why nothing really changed yet. But when I recognized the problem, I repented, and the change in ministry began.

I remember a brother I met in Sacramento about twenty years ago or so, and I asked him a question about ministry and how to do better, and he said tell the Lord every morning that you are available for whatever he wanted to do in you, when I did that things began to transform my walk with him again my prayer life changed and understanding increased about God and his workings and his heart.

Things started happening like the scripture that I read the night before. I would use it to minister the next day to someone (note this is when I was first starting to preach in the Baptist Church) all things work together for your good. Romans 8:28-29 you are being conformed to Christ's image this was when I had a lot of religion in me and didn't know it.

Then years later with religion in me, I went to Southern California with David Dolve, a close friend of mine. We were there to meet his spiritual dad at that time. His name is Dave Duel from Colorado. My life was changed forever when I met him, and now, he's my spiritual dad. Dave is as free as anyone I have ever seen in my life. We met with him at a conference in Banning, Californiawhere he was preaching and ministering. At one of the meetings we were attending in the morning, Dave told a story about a man standing up in a meeting and said to Dave, "Man of God, you have a word for me and I'm not leaving until you give to me." Dave ministered to him. About one hour later in the next meeting that morning, before I knew what was happening, I jumped up, and I told Dave, whom I had just met, that he had a word for me and I was not going home without it. He said brother I sure do and fifteen minutes later he called me out and said something to me that freed me forever. I quote what he said, "Brother, you came down here with all that religion and you're going home completely free." He laid hands on me, and I hit the floor groaning and I was completely free from a religious spirit. Thank God I'm free indeed, amen.

Much more, at the prayer retreat spoken of earlier, my life changed. Now after being in ministry for twenty-two years, what changed was the way I see ministry, free from religion or in a box.

I felt like I had to do it this way or the way I saw someone else doing it. God called all of us in our own uniqueness and with our own personality. We are different from each other. Surely you will do things that your spiritual father does, but that helps you get to who God called you to be. Dave is my spiritual father and I love him, but I know he's helped me let the true John H. Lucas Jr. come forth, for it is Christ in me the hope of glory. I stopped trying to be someone else because I have my own identity in Christ.

Psalm 139:13-16 states, "For you created my inmost being; you knit me together in my mother's womb. I praise you because I am fearfully and wonderfully made; your works are wonderful, I know that full well. My frame was not hidden from you when I was made in the secret place. When I was woven together in the depths of the earth, your eyes saw my unformed body. All the days ordained for me were written in your book before one of them came to be."

This is a powerful revelation of our identity, especially if we are struggling with who we are. The world is in this quandary. People are trying to be someone God never intended them to be. They look at sports, movies, images, etc. And that is one reason they have America idle.

It's not just a show but it's a lifestyle that God is not pleased with at all.

More verses will help us as we meditate on them and see yourself.

Not just the apostles and pastors and so on, but you.

Jeremiah 29:11

"For I know the plans I have for you," declares the Lord. "Plans to prosper you and not to harm you. Plans to give you hope and a future."

Ephesians 1:4-5

For he chose us in him before the creation of the world to be holy and blameless in his sight. In love he predestined us to be adopted as his sons through Jesus Christ, in accordance with his pleasure and will.

Ephesians 2:10

For we are God's workmanship, created in Christ Jesus to do good works, which God prepared in advance for us to do.

Declare this:

God knows the plans he has for me.

God chose me.

I am God's workmanship.

This will help you to realize who you are and who He is in you.

Repeat this as often as you need to. What a glorious liberty we have in Christ. Whom the son has set free is free indeed. John 8:36 if the son therefore shall make you free, ye shall be free indeed.

This is the key that brought more miracles.

In prayer, I begin to ask God in the morning, especially when I am ministering that day, "Lord, what are you doing today that I can do with you or that I can be a part of?" And then I would wait for the answer. I always try to remember to get a pen and paper to write down things he would say, but sometimes he would have to tell me to get a pen and paper.

I started getting words of knowledge to give to people, places to go, people to see, directions for ministry, and other things not yet to be released—to hold them for the timing of God.

Knowing when to release the words publicly or in private, corporately or tell the leader of the congregation or ministry, is very critical for the success of ministry.

I have many stories about my failures in ministry. Doing it my way and what I thought God wanted. We must be like David, a man after God's own heart. He didn't have God's heart, but he was constantly running after God's heart. David was hungry for what God wanted. He was not perfect, but this was one thing God liked about David.

David was a worshipper, which also tells you a lot about what pleases God—true worshippers. He liked David so much, the Bible says that David's house will be rebuilt as the house or tent of worship. Acts 15:16 After this I will return, and will build again the tabernacle of David, which is fallen down; and I will build again the ruins thereof, and I will set it up.

I remember one day I had so much zeal that I tried to raise this paralyzed lady out of a wheelchair, and I used the scripture. I said, "Silver and gold I don't have, etc. Rise up and walk." I reached down and stood her up, and nothing happened. I struggled with this dead weight, and I got her back in the wheelchair, embarrassed. I said, "Lord, why didn't you heal her?" And he said, "I didn't tell you to do that." I repented and prayed more about what he was doing that day and on what he says and do what I see him doing.

I heard someone speaking one day on TBN about Jesus saying what his Father is saying, and he said that Jesus did not speak in Greek, but Hebrew. And when he said "I only say what I hear him saying," he was actually saying "when I hear him think it, I say it." This could be true because he and his Father are one.

My brother-in-law passed away two years ago, and my wife and I tried to raise him from the dead to no avail. I again asked the Lord, "Why didn't you raise him up?" He again said, "I didn't tell you to do this." As you can see, I haven't arrived, but I'm running hard after God. (Psalm 63:8) My soul followeth hard after thee: thy right hand upholdeth me.

Striving for perfection and seeking him early—all these are necessary. Thank God there is now no condemnation. Read Romans 8:1.

Don't be afraid of FAILURE. It is a key to success.

As we mature in Christ, we will better walk in true obedience and faith. One day, I was in the shower, and I asked God what it is that I don't understand about faith, and he said "obedience." If *faith* is a verb, then it is an action word. You can't have faith without works because the Bible says that is dead faith. So you need to act on that faith before you really have faith. Some people never get anywhere because of fear, the opposite of faith.

At a meeting in Sacramento that I attended, Apostle Fredrick Price was the speaker, and he said belief is not enough. "I have a Bentley, and I can get on the hood of that car and believe I can drive it away. But nothing is going to happen until I get off the hood of that car, take the keys and open the door, put the keys in the ignition, turn the keys and start the car, put the transmission into drive, and push on the gas. I must do something for faith to manifest."

What I'm saying is don't let failure keep you from moving out and doing what God has purposed for you to do before the foundation of the world. Use your failures as Thomas Edison did. It was recorded that Edison had failed a thousand times trying to invent the light bulb, but he said, "I have not failed a thousand times. I have successfully discovered one thousand ways not to make the light bulb."

In other words he never gave up. Have you?

Let me ask you a question. "What if the secret to success was failure?" In another book, many of us could write that one, but the scripture tells us we can do all things through Christ who strengthens us. Let's take a look at the Amplified Version.

I have strength for all things in Christ who empowers me [I am ready for anything and equal to anything through him who [a] infuses inner strength into me; I am [b] self-sufficient in Christ's sufficiency]. Glory to God! What a powerful word for all of us. God is not looking for a super saint, but one who is has a heart after his will and purposes, now. And as Paul says in Philippians 3:13, "Forget those things which are behind you, and pressing forth unto those things which are before you."

Don't give up; you can do it. The box is open. Now it's time to let God out. Keep reading.

Chapter Five

Signs of the grace
First testimony

John Lucas Jr.: Yehudit, greetings in the name above all names. Here is the testimony I shared with you and some additional information I received last night. All glory to Abba. Sunday night, the 22nd of April 2012, we were in our normal Sunday night times-of-refreshing-in-the-presence-of-the-Lord portion of the service.

And as we were having worship, the glory was beginning to set in, and I was caught up in the spirit. I was taken into the brain of one of our members who had just had brain surgery to remove a tumor. As I was going through her brain in the spirit, I went to the area that they had removed the tumor, and I saw a spot and I scratched it off. The Lord said I'm going to the root of this thing, and we traveled to an area deep into her brain and I saw another spot, and the Lord sprinkled that spot with water and it was gone, just like that. Then I saw the trauma from the surgery leave, and I knew that her headaches were gone. This was about 6:30 p.m.

The next morning, I called her and shared with her the experience I had. To my surprise, she was sitting outside on a windy day, and she said that all the headaches were gone the night before and she was surprised that she had no setbacks from sitting outside on a very windy day. To God be the glory. Last night—April 25, 2012—she came to the Bible study for the first time since having the operation. She said, to my amazement, that she had gone back to the doctor for a checkup. The doctor told her that when they operated, they might have left a spot of the tumor in, not intentionally. But it was not dangerous to her. The tumor was tested and had some disease, but she had no signs of having it through observation. The patient is doing well, and again I say, "To Abba be all the glory for the things he's doing."

[11:43:36 a.m.] John Lucas Jr.: I can't explain it, but I know that there are different dimensions that God can take us into, as we can be transported from one place to another as we see in the Bible as Jesus walked through the door or wall through another realm or dimension in the spirit.

If someone tells you a story like this, you would say you are crazy, but is anything too hard for God? Is his hand short that he can't reach anywhere?

Matt. 19:26 states, "But Jesus beheld *them,* and said unto them, with men this is impossible; but with God all things are possible."

Let me set the picture the night this happened. We have our night services, and we call them "Times of Refreshing in the Presence of the Lord" (Acts 3:19). This particular night the worship was glorious and I was caught up in the spirit. I immediately entered Sister Sheila's brain. I knew who it was and why I was there. As I looked around, I saw a spot near the back of her brain near the medulla oblongata and I scratched it off with my finger. Then Jesus appeared to my left and he said, "Let's go in deeper and get to the root of this problem." Sheila had just had surgery four to five days prior to this encounter. So Jesus and I went in deeper and we saw another spot. This one was bigger and he just simply sprinkled some water on it and it went away immediately. At that time, I knew in my spirit that the entire trauma that she had reported to me that week was gone in an instant. The sprinkled water made every headache pain and discomfort disappear. At the service when I came to myself I almost couldn't wait until the next day to call her and ask her how she felt. When I did call the next day, to my surprise she was sitting outside on a very windy day with no problems at all and she said that night all the headaches and pressure was gone. I didn't ask her the exact time that happened, but I think I know praise God. Because of the operation the family couldn't come to service for a week, but that Wednesday they came as previously stated and told me that Tuesday she had a checkup after the operation. During the first checkup the doctor told her after she examined her that they had done a biopsy on the tumor they removed. It had some disease, but she showed no visible signs of it. The doctor said when they did the operation they might have unintentionally left a spot of the tumor in there. Just last week Sheila had another CAT scan, and it showed that there was no spot or anything other than a perfect brain. No spots or tumors, praise our faithful God outside of the normal box. We forget God is sovereign. Why God did it this way, I don't know and I bet Sheila doesn't care because she's completely made free by the power of God. I've also noticed that before the operation she was slow of speech sometimes. But not now, she teaches Sunday school and preaches too! Wow! What an awesome God we serve!

> 1 Cor. 1:27 But God hath chosen the foolish things of the world to confound the wise; and God hath chosen the weak things of the world to confound the things which are mighty;
>
> 1 Cor. 1:28 And base things of the world, and things which are despised, hath God chosen, *yea,* and things which are not, to bring to nought things that are:
>
> 1 Cor. 1:29 That no flesh should glory in his presence. (KJV)

Let's look at the Amplified Version. [27] [no] for God selected (deliberately chose) what in the world is foolish to put the wise to shame, and what the world calls weak to put the strong to shame. ²⁸ And God also selected (deliberately chose) what in the world is lowborn *and* insignificant and branded *and* treated with contempt, even the things that are nothing, that he might depose *and* bring to nothing the things that are, ²⁹ So that no mortal man should [have pretense for glorying and] boast in the presence of God.

In verse 27 it says he deliberately chose what the world sees as foolish, things, people, situation, etc., so that no flesh can glory in His presence. I believe God is trying to send a revival that will turn the world upside down. But it won't look like and be like anything we have seen or heard. It will truly be a new thing.

Isa. 43:18 Remember ye not the former things, neither consider the things of old.

> Isa. 43:19 Behold, I will do a new thing; now it shall spring forth; shall ye not know it? I will even make a way in the wilderness, *and* rivers in the desert.

This scripture is powerful. It says forget the former things, neither remember the things or ways you use to do things of old. The problem I discovered is that in our services we would play a certain song or CD and the power of God would move mightily. Because that happened last Sunday, we would play that song again and expect the same thing to happen. It may or may not happen because the Lord taught us to find out what he's doing, what pleases him today, what he wants to hear, does he want worship only or praise only, or does he want us to wait on him with no music at all. This takes a deep level of obedience. The norm is to prepare some songs. I say that's OK, but check with him before you hit one note or sing one song. I believe many are walking in this now. This is where you see constant signs and wonders, and miracles that are unusual in nature. I mean miracles that come in unusual ways.

Amos 3:7 says, "Surely the Lord will do nothing until he has revealed his secrets to his servants, the prophets." I keep getting hints of revival. I attend a prayer meeting every Wednesday in the Roseville House of Prayer. We pray for revival and for the local pastors. One day, the Lord sent the pastor to where Evans Roberts started the Welsh Revival. Pastor Francs from the Rock of Roseville has a real passion for revival. He said that we too can reach one person, one church at a time, and let it begin in us. The prophets are seeing it coming. Take a look at the Elijah List reports.

This testimony is one that should be common and in some places. It is my prayer that God opens the eyes of the church-at-large and we all look the same, act the same, and set this world on fire with the glory of God. In this I mean that we don't have to look or act the same but be of the same spirit and mind.

Matt. 10:7 And as ye go, preach, saying, the kingdom of heaven is at hand.

Matt. 10:8 Heal the sick, cleanse the lepers, raise the dead, cast out devils: freely ye have received, freely give.

As you go to the supermarket, to the hospital, wash your clothes, etc. Go.

Chapter Six

Signs of the Grace Testimony Two

Daddy, here is my write up of the Outpouring 2012:

We had our scheduled Outpouring Conference in January 2012. And here goes my testimony:

Every year there is always excitement in our hearts as we know that God has something different to do in our midst. This time it was so amazing, there are no exact words to describe the mighty move of God.

On the first day when we started with the praise and worship, we sensed the mighty move of God. And as our speaker, Apostle John Lucas stands, he let us sing the song "I Love You Lord." As we sing it the glory of God began to fall and we can't contain it. We were shaking; some were crying, and even slain in the spirit. God's presence is so tangible. Amazing!

There was a period of time used for the impartation of gifts and those who have received a gift began to exercise the gift immediately. God is great! Our speakers called many up front and let them prophesy as the spirit instructed them or to speak forth healing. They trained us to be more sensitive to the unction of the Holy Spirit and to listen to the voice of God and do what he says. Truly, if you want more of God, he will satisfy you.

The services lasted a long time. We enjoyed God's presence so much, we didn't notice the time. Even as we went home, we were still high in spirit. Hallelujah!

I couldn't understand it, but I personally got a stomachache and I didn't know what to do. I even called for Mom Tina to pray for me because I couldn't bear the pain, but nothing happened. The next day, I told Dad John about my experience. He told me God was doing something in me.

The next day, more infilling and we just received and received what the Holy Spirit was pouring out to us, preparing us for the assignment for his glory. Wow! The intensity of God's glory was greater and thicker as we went deeper into his presence, while our speakers from time to time declared our gifts and callings. We did nothing but remained alert and sensitive to the move of God. You don't want to miss anything that the Lord is doing. Many gifts and callings were proclaimed and they also gave us warning to be on guard and not to slack off because the anointing we received will not be taken away from us. Glory to

God! When the service was over, we mingled as we usually do, but the move of the Spirit was not yet finished. Apostle John was talking to someone and Pastora Gina was there with him. Suddenly Apostle John turned to her, and the Spirit of God fell on her—she was being filled. We were there to assist her, and we were also filled. Later on, Pastora stood straight up and began calling us one by one. Those who were called were asked to stay in the middle of the room, and without us knowing it, there was an arrangement that was formed. As they interpreted it, it's like a ship with Pastora as the commander and those who were called were lined up in two rows, wow! It was a powerful day for each one!

Now when the final day of the conference came, we were asked to wear a white top and also declared that we fast from 6:00 a.m. to 2:00 p.m. In the very morning you could sense the holiness of God in that place. Everybody was in a white T-shirt or blouse. It was so peaceful. They said it would be a commissioning which we usual do at the end of the conference, but it did not turn out that way. God's way is perfect. It was such a glorious, awesome service that we ended the service at 4:00 p.m. instead of 2:00 p.m. Many things happened that day. That's when Apostle John ministered to Jocelyn by imparting gifts. Then she was slain in the spirit. When she got up, wow, amazing things happened. The power of God was so strong! She ministered, she laid hands on the sick, and they were healed instantly. We were in awe of God's power upon her as more miracles were happening. We recognized that she had received the gift of healing.

We ended this great service and conference gloriously and victoriously. We do not have enough words, and they are inadequate to describe everything we had experienced and felt in this glorious, amazing conference. Our God is more than amazing, more than wonderful and much glorious!

We thank God for the lives of our two daddies Apostle John and Prophet Ray for being with us. They shared everything they received from God. With all these great things, there is only one who is worthy to receive the highest praise, honor, glory, adoration and thanks, our only most high God our Father in Jesus's name.

By Meriam Fernandez, Hong Kong, JTR Church.

This is a testimony from one of the spiritual daughters in Hong Kong at a church called Jesus the True Redeemer International Fellowship, Hong Kong or JTR.

I have been going to JTR for four years now. The first time was 2009. I took a team of two people with me. It was so exciting because of the level of hunger the people had for God. I experienced things unlike anything I had ever seen. Being a missionary, I had traveled exclusively to the Philippines every year since 2001, but had never seen the hunger that I saw in Hong Kong.

The domestic workers there were hurting because they are not treated well by their bosses. They are treated less favorably since most of them are believers, some Catholic. When we travel, the date is scheduled, and they will fast and pray for months prior to our arrival.

The expectation is great, and the atmosphere is charged to a level for miracles and many signs and wonders. Many occur during the January Outpouring Conference. I had jet lag like never before but the glory of God caused us to flow with the Holy Ghost. Remember, when I wake up in the morning, I will ask the Holy Ghost, "What are you going to do today in the service?" I get paper and write it down.

The first day, he revealed to me that he wanted to impart the gift of faith to Jocelyn, one of the leaders of JTR. You have to understand that Jocelyn is very shy and reserved, unless she is leading worship. But if she's ministering, she's very shy. Well, the Lord wanted to impart this gift to her. While this doesn't sound so unusual, it's the way God wanted me to impart to her that was so unusual. Now stay in the Spirit while I say this. God showed me kissing her on the cheeks, forehead, and lips. Well, I wondered about this myself and questioned the Lord how come I couldn't just lay hands on her.

Let me go back a little in the story. Remember I have a spiritual father, and he imparted to me some gifts. Well, my dad kisses people and they are healed and delivered. Jesus did miracles many different ways, not always the same. I don't kiss everyone I see either, but it's out of the box because the people who get healed of cancer won't argue over a kiss. They don't care because they are healed and set free.

This story might offend many, but I'm not worried about that. I must obey the Lord so the spirit of religion can be broken off the church forever. Don't judge me.

When I was put in this position, I had to either obey or disobey the Lord. Obedience is better than sacrifice (1 Samuel 15:22). I must say this, I'm not saying for you to go around kissing people because you read a book. But I am saying that however God wants to use you, don't put God in the box of religion or fear.

I decided to obey God—his sheep knows his voice and he won't listen or obey a stranger's voice. What I did was not fully obeying the Lord. I felt that I should not offend anyone, so I kissed her on the cheeks and forehead. Instead of kissing her on the lips, I called Pastora Gina over to cover her mouth, and I kissed the back of pastor's hand. Jocelyn was slain in the spirit and we waited to see if this was God. She got up and immediately had a word of knowledge. She called out people's diseases, and with great boldness, she must have ministered to about twenty-five people or more. Pastora came to me as Jocelyn was ministering and said I have never seen her like this. She was always so reserved and shy, but not anymore. After Jocelyn stopped for a while, I ministered for about fifteen minutes. Jocelyn was behind me and said she had more. I gave the mic to her and she gave more words of knowledge. I had a rash on my back and I got in line and she prayed for me. I was slain in the spirit and as I lay there, the Lord said when you kissed the back of Pastora's hand; she received some of that anointing. Afterward, I stood on my feet and told Pastora what the Lord said, she said that she knew it when she turned away from me.

Now what happened next will surely get the religious in an uproar. Pastora immediately called one of the young ladies over and slapped her on her right cheek with her left hand, and the lady was slain and was set free of double mindedness. But wait, not done yet. Pastor's husband, Pastor Arnel, said he wanted her to slap him to be free from some things in his past, and the church went wild with joy and laughter. Pastora didn't want to do it but obeyed and when she slapped Pastor Arnel with that same left hand.

Let me pause here and interject some important info to the story. Fifteen years before this, Pastora and Pastor Arnel had some marital problems that I won't mention here. This plays a great part into how hard she wanted to slap him.

As she drew back to slap him she was happy but a little reserved because of the Filipino culture. She hit him with all she had, and he was slain in the spirit. What amazed me was every woman in the service was completely set free from marital problems and forgave their husbands in the Philippines. Wow, the glory of God filled the place and we praised God for an hour after that, singing and making melody in our hearts to the Lord of glory for the things he had done.

By Meriam Fernandez, Hong Kong, JTR Church

Can I explain it, no one said to us here in Sacramento that the Lord said to them that we can't take credit when someone is healed and we can't take the blame when they're not, where the spirit is Lord there is liberty, freedom.

As I'm writing this book in Home of Peace in Oakland, California, I'm sensing that there are many people who have been in bondage to a system that does not promote freedom, but has rules and regulations that choke your God-given talents and gifts. Let's look at a scripture that keeps ringing in my spirit.

Col. 2:4 and this I say, lest any man should beguile you with enticing words.

Col. 2:5 for though I be absent in the flesh, yet am I with you in the spirit, joying and beholding your order, and the stedfastness of your faith in Christ.

Col. 2:6 as ye have therefore received Christ Jesus the Lord, *so* walk ye in him:

Col. 2:7 rooted and built up in him, and stablished in the faith, as ye have been taught, abounding therein with thanksgiving.

Col. 2:8 beware lest any man spoil you through philosophy and vain deceit, after the tradition of men, after the rudiments of the world, and not after Christ.

Col. 2:9 for in him dwelleth all the fulness of the Godhead bodily.

Col. 2:10 and ye are complete in him, which is the head of all principality and power: (KJV)

Now the Amplified Version,

[4] I say this in order that no one may mislead *and* delude you by plausible *and* persuasive *and* attractive arguments *and* beguiling speech.

[5] for though I am away from you in body, yet I am with you in spirit, delighted at the sight of your [standing shoulder to shoulder in such] orderly array and the firmness *and* the solid front *and* steadfastness of your faith in Christ [that [e] leaning of the entire human personality on him in absolute trust and confidence in his power, wisdom, and goodness].

[6] as you have therefore received Christ, [even] Jesus the Lord, [so] walk (regulate your lives and conduct yourselves) in union with *and* conformity to him.

[7] have the roots [of your being] firmly *and* deeply planted [in him, fixed and founded in him], being continually built up in him, becoming increasingly more confirmed *and* established in the faith, just as you were taught, and abounding *and* overflowing in it with thanksgiving.

8 see to it that no one carries you off as spoil *or* makes you yourselves captive by his so-called philosophy *and* intellectualism and vain deceit (idle fancies and plain nonsense), following human tradition (men's ideas of the material rather than the spiritual world), just crude notions following the rudimentary *and* elemental teachings of the universe and disregarding [the teachings of] Christ (the Messiah).

9 for in him the whole fullness of deity (the Godhead) continues to dwell in bodily form [giving complete expression of the divine nature].

10 and you [f] are in him, made full *and* having come to fullness of life [in Christ you too are filled with the Godhead—Father, Son, and Holy Spirit—and reach full spiritual stature]. And he is the head of all rule and authority [of every angelic principality and power].

Don't let anyone beguile you, let's look at that word: g3884

Παραλογίζομαι

Paralogizomai

Par-al-og-id'-zom-ahee

From g3844 and g3049; to *misreckon*, that is, *delude:*—beguile, deceive.

(from the Strong's Concordance)

Notice this is a compound word

Para meaning g3844

Para

Par-ah

A primary preposition; properly *near*, that is, (with genitive case) *from beside* (literally or figuratively), (with dative case) *at* (or *in*) the *vicinity* of (objectively or subjectively), **G3049**

Logizomai

Log-id'-zom-ahee

Middle voice from g3056; to *take an inventory*, that is, *estimate* (literally or figuratively):—conclude, (ac-) count (of), + despise, esteem, impute, lay, number, reason, reckon, suppose, think (on).

Which is saying that to take an inventory near you to deceive you, people near you will try and tell you things that are not biblically based, but they are traditions of man. Jesus told the religious that their traditions make his word of no effect.

God is still healing, delivering, and saving people no matter how it looks in the world. The Lord of Glory is still on the throne. Say, "Lord, take me out of the boxes of man."

I must say something here. I'm not talking about being in rebellion to your leadership, submit to authority.

Sometimes we think we have arrived, but wait on your ministry. God will let you know when His timing is for you.

Chapter Seven

Signs of the Grace Testimony Three

Trip to Hong Kong at the Jesus the True Redeemer Ministries International Limited Church:

Daddy, below is my write-up from the Outpouring 2011—Equipping for Service.

Our God is greater! Awesome in power.

Truly, our God is never lacking the great things for his children who hunger and thirst for him.

The mighty move of God continues since last year's outpouring. Everybody was excited for this year's outpouring for we know that greater things will happen. So we prayed and prepared ourselves. The very Sunday when (Dad) Apostle John arrived, we got a bonus from God. While we were just sitting and sharing, Dad was urged to minister and prayed specific prayers.

For the fatherless, God's presence was so powerful that everyone fell where they were, overwhelmed with the Father's love. What an awesome evening and everyone went home so blessed. Hallelujah! Dad also shared with us about following instructions. Then Thursday, the three-day conference commenced. Personally, I don't know how well I described everything we had experienced in the conference. Some were really indescribable. We had learned that if you want to be equipped for service, then you need a change, "change it, and implement change!" As I look back from last year, I've seen change in us, and we have grown up in the Lord.

We now know how to handle or manage ourselves when there is unusual mighty move of God.

Of the Holy Spirit, unlike last year, we screamed. We didn't know what to do. There is chaos and riot in our midst. Ha. Ha. Ha. Following instructions is the very message in this outpouring in order to be equipped for service, to be more sensitive and hear from the Spirit, and it's deeper. Surrender, trust, and obedience pays a reward of righteousness.

Also a vital role: The second day was a glorious one. God's healing power was greatly displayed. Different kinds of body pains and sicknesses were healed, feet were straightened out, and there were also inner healings. One of the major healings that happened was the complete healing of our sister with stage 3 cancer. The doctors couldn't accept and couldn't believe what they had found out in the x-ray result and said it was so embarrassing on their part because no cancer cells were found. Hallelujah! Glory to God! Our God is a God of miracles and with him nothing is impossible! It was also on this day that there was an impartation of gifts and application of gifts that were received.

The presence of God was so tangible and His love enveloped everyone, especially when we sing the song "Bind Us Together." We had such an amazing and awesome time that we couldn't end the meeting. We finished past 7:00 p.m. in the evening, but we were supposed to be finished at 5:00 p.m. Everybody went home filled and rejoicing. The last day of the conference was intended for commissioning, but it went differently as the Spirit led the apostle and prophet to do a prophetic gesture with the use of the red cloth. Oh, it was so glorious and powerful. The cloth was laid over our heads as we were standing. The apostle and prophet first laid it on Pastora Jina and Brother Arnel, then Pastora laid it on the leaders, and then on everyone. The glory of God was so powerful that when the cloth was laid on your head, you couldn't contain the presence and power of God. Some saw visions, some were baptized with the Holy Ghost, and some saw heaven open. Everyone experienced the awesome power and greatness of God. Glorious! Awesome! Magnificent! Glory! People had deeper commitments to God happened and they were transformed, never to be the same again. With all this, we are so thankful to the Lord and with you our dads, Prophet Ray and Apostle John, for your unselfish love and help to us.

To the Most High God our Heavenly Father, we give you all the glory, honor, praise, adoration, and thanksgiving in Jesus name Amen.

Miss and love you, Daddy,

Daughter Meriam FL

In this testimony, I want to point out two parts that are significant to this book and the uniqueness of taking God out of the box and seeing his faithfulness to his word.

But first, I remembered a prophetic word that Che Ahn gave me at the Family Christian Center in Orangevale, California—a wonderful place of worship and anointing. This was about ten years ago, and I was attending a glorious conference, and as I went for prayer, he said, "John, you will see miracles in your ministry." And surely, I have seen some awesome things in the last ten years, praise God.

First point: you notice in this chapter there was a lady healed of stage 3 cancer. Let me tell you about the circumstances surrounding this great miracle

I arrived in Hong Kong on a Sunday morning, and the conference wasn't scheduled to start until Thursday that week. So I had time to rest and get over jet lag. I told my spiritual daughters who picked me up at the airport I would go to sleep, and I would call someone if I got hungry. I didn't want to go by the church because I knew if I did, it would create a disturbance because they would be so glad to see me—that it would break their concentration from the speaker that Sunday. So I slept for about four hours, and I woke up when Meriam Fernandez, one of my daughters, called me and asked me if I was ready to eat. I said yes, and we went to the mall for dinner. After we ate, I said, "Nothing is going on at the church, so let's stop by for a few minutes." But to my surprise, Pastor Arnel was teaching a homiletics class, and when I went in, it disrupted the class for five or so minutes. I felt bad afterward. Pastor Arnel said he started to stop the class, but thank God he didn't.

So I sat in the back, away from everyone, and the class ended in about thirty minutes. Everyone came and formed a horseshoe with chairs facing me, and all of a sudden, the Spirit started moving. Some of the young ladies came and hugged me, saying that they loved me and that they never had a dad. I asked the rest of the ladies who didn't have a dad growing up. About twelve raised their hands. I waved my hands at them, and they all went out in the Spirit.

What happened next was so unusual. The Lord said to kiss this lady with a bald head, and I said no twice. He said, "Kiss her on the top of her bald head, and her name is Tess." I didn't know what was going on with her, but I figured she had cancer. I called her over to me and kissed her on her head, and she was slain in the Spirit and was set free instantly from stage 3 breast cancer. Wow.

Two days later, I told Pastora Jina to have her go to the bathroom and check herself. So she and the Pastora went in, and we all heard a scream for joy. The cancer was so bad that she had a hole in her breast, and it was seeping a fluid out. That had all dried up. To God be the glory!

Pastora and the prophet and I were due to go to the Philippines after the outpouring in Hong Kong, to run an outpouring in two cities in the Philippines. The day we were getting ready to leave, someone called me and asked me if I had heard about Sister Tess. I said no, and they said they would let her call me and tell me what happened.

Now I couldn't really wait too long, but she finally called and said that the doctor wanted to check and see if they needed to keep going with the chemo. They gave her an X-ray, and when they got the results, they called her in and said, "We owe you an apology. We told you that you had cancer, and now we can't find it. What did you do with it?"

Wow! I was in a hotel room, and I ran out the door, down the hallway, and the Chinese people were looking at me like I had gone crazy. They did not understand, but my God is so awesome, I didn't care what they thought. Amen.

I saw Tess this year, and she said "Dad, I'm free" with the most incredible smile in the world. She trusted in God, and he showed himself faithful. Great is thy faithfulness.

Tess was told by the doctors she had cancer, and she laughed so hard that the doctors thought she was crazy. They called the pastor of the church and told him that they just told her she had cancer and she was laughing. What the doctor didn't understand was she had been praying and reading the word in Isaiah 53:5.

> Isa. 53:5 but he *was* wounded for our transgressions, *he was* bruised for our iniquities: the chastisement of our peace *was* upon him; and with his stripes we are healed.

She hung on to this word, not fearing or believing the report of the doctors, and God showed up on time—praise him, hallelujah.

The second point: the red cloth. In 2009, we were in the Philippines, and the Lord said to me to get a bell and a red cloth and lie on it under my mattress in the hotel room. The cloth was four feet wide by twelve feet long. It was not for the Philippines, but for Hong Kong. Everyone on the team was asking me what this is for. I said I didn't know, and I just obeyed God.

So when we were leaving the Philippines for Hong Kong, we were at the airport and discovered I had left the cloth under my mattress at the hotel. A policeman at the airport let me use his cell phone, and a friend brought it to me on a motorcycle. Amen. We got to Hong Kong, and the second day of the meeting, I used that cloth to minister. The Lord told me not to leave the cloth, but take it home.

At home, my wife and another minister cut it in half and then cut the half into smaller pieces. In 2011, the Lord told me to take that larger section back to Hong Kong, and before that day's meeting, the Lord showed me in the morning what to do with it.

This is also great. He told me to lay it on all the leaders for an impartation. I didn't do all of it. Pastor Arnel and Pastora Jina lay it on all the other leaders, and it was so awesome, some didn't want to let the cloth go. This lasted for a couple of hours or more as everyone was receiving a deep impartation with a deeper commitment to the Lord and their leaders. As Meriam said, some had visions and all kinds of manifestations as the glory overtook them. This can only happen when you know God's voice and obey it, to God be the glory for the things he's done and will do in and through you.

Chapter Eight

More signs of this Grace Testimony Four

Testimony to God's Healing Power
Glory Healing Conference, Yuba City, CA

April 22, 2011

This happened during the Glory Healing Conference hosted by Joy Gartman in Yuba City. At the end of the night, Pastor John Lucas called for those with numerous physical needs to come forward for prayer. One of the things he called out was a hearing problem in the right ear. Gail asked me if I was going to go up. I said, "Go up for what?" She said Pastor Lucas had called for those who had a hearing problem in their right ear. I didn't hear him. Pretty much sums that up.

I went up for prayer, and the glory of God hit me like a freight train. *Gail said it looked like lightning struck me!* I've heard about people being thrown back and falling under the power of God, but this was the first time I had experienced the glory in this manner. Pastor Lucas spoke over me, and he did not touch me or lay hands on me. God and God alone touched me, and I lost all control. I started shaking, was thrown back, and went down. I lost all my dignity that night.

As I lay fallen under the power of the glory of God, there was warmth going through my right ear. I felt the sensation of a draining, but not in the physical sense. There was no physical discharge from my ear but, rather, a spiritual discharge. I knew that the scar tissue in my ear was being removed and that my hearing was being restored. I didn't know how long it would take to fully manifest, but I was healed! Praise God. By the next day, I could hear again.

We returned for the Saturday night session, and as I greeted Pastor Lucas, I couldn't help but declare that as the Verizon commercial says, "I can hear you now."

Glory to God for healing me.

—Chuck Pyle.

Joy Gartman and I were having these glory meetings in Yuba City for about five or six months. They were glorious, and the worship was awesome too. We tag teamed. It was a great flow every night, and we saw bona fide miracles every night of our meeting.

Chuck Pyle's miracle was very different because, as I said previously, the Lord would show me the morning of the services what was going to happen—or, better said, what he was going to do. That night, I had about twelve words of knowledge, and I released them and sat down, and Joy took over. But I had only sat down a few minutes, and the Lord said someone had a right-ear problem. I went to Joy and told her, and we released the words. At first, no one came forward. Then Chuck came forth, and he told me about the problem he had for some time. Now the Holy Spirit hit him, and he was down on the floor, groaning. The next night, he came up and gave his testimony. We praised God for his healing.

Remember the other words that were given? Well, some of the words were given, but some people never moved. One month later, we had come back for another meeting, and after the meeting, Joy was talking to a middle-aged lady on the front row. I walked over, and Joy said that when we were up there a month ago, this lady was sitting there when the words were given. She told her girlfriend that Pastor Lucas had given three things that were wrong with her, but she wouldn't move. When she went to the doctor for her checkup, she found out she was delivered from all three things. She had a cancerous tumor and two other things. She was completely made whole by the power of God.

The Bible says that Jesus went about doing good, healing all that were oppressed of the devil, because God was with him (Acts10:38b).

One thing that concerns me is people who say they want to be healed. However, when the "power to heal" is there they don't want to move. That lady said, "I don't know why I'm not going up there." Thank God for his grace. He healed her anyway. Out of the box of what we think should happen. We know that the enemy wants them to stay sick or infirmed.

I see the same things overseas, and that is a shame. Proverbs 11:2 states that "*when* pride cometh, then cometh shame: but with the lowly *is* wisdom." Shame is a product of pride. We shouldn't be ashamed of the Gospel. It is God's good pleasure to give us the kingdom, which includes the healing virtue that Jesus gave us with the authority to do greater works. But there's something else I've seen, and it is a sad thing. Some people don't want to be healed because their disability check might stop.

When I was young in the ministry, I called out a person in the church and told him what I saw in his body. He whispered to me, "Don't pray now. I have to get my checks set up first."

That's deep! My prayer is like what Catherine Kulhman said, "Let this be the night everyone is healed." Amen.

One of the things that God is teaching me about words of knowledge is that some people are not comfortable with this type of ministry. They have had hands laid on them so much, they can't receive deliverance any other way. But this book is about

God's faithfulness and the boxes we have put him in. Jesus healed in many ways, and not the same way all the time. He would say, "Be thou made whole." He would spit on the ground and put mud in someone's eyes, or he would speak the word only. Let's look at this scripture.

Matt. 8:5 and when Jesus was entered into Capernaum, there came unto him a centurion, beseeching him,

Matt. 8:6 and saying, Lord, my servant lieth at home sick of the palsy, grievously tormented.

Matt. 8:7 and Jesus saith unto him, I will come and heal him.

Matt. 8:8 the centurion answered and said, Lord, I am not worthy that thou shouldest come under my roof: but speak the word only, and my servant shall be healed.

Matt. 8:9 for I am a man under authority, having soldiers under me: and I say to this *man,* go, and he goeth; and to another, come, and he cometh; and to my servant, do this, and he doeth *it.*

Matt. 8:10 when Jesus heard *it,* he marvelled, and said to them that followed, verily I say unto you, I have not found so great faith, no, not in Israel.

This man's servant was not even with the centurion.

This means Jesus didn't lay hands on him.

Jesus offered to come to the centurion's house. That was one way to heal. But something that touched Jesus happened in verse 9. The man knew what kind authority that Jesus had. He said, "I am a man under authority having soldiers under me, and I have people under me and they do what I tell them to do." But verse 8 is showing how much faith he had in Jesus's authority. This is one of the things that God is dealing with the body of Christ about. Not only do we have to walk in that authority, we have to have good character and good integrity so that people will have that same faith in you as an ambassador of Christ.

Eph. 6:20 for which I am an ambassador in bonds: that therein I may speak boldly, as I ought to speak.

An ambassador is one who *acts as a representative. In this case, we represent Christ in character and in action.*

Our lives must line up with Christ's ways and his attributes.

Attributes: a quality, property, or characteristic of someone or something

OSon of the living God. Jesus said, "If you've seen me, you seen the father, and they are one" (John 14:9; John 17:11, 22).

> John 14:9 Jesus saith unto him, have I been so long time with you, and yet hast thou not known me, Philip? He that hath seen me hath seen the father; and how sayest thou *then,* shew us the father?

> John 17:11 and now I am no more in the world, but these are in the world, and I come to thee. Holy Father, keep through thine own name those whom thou hast given me, that they may be one, as we *are.*

> John 17:22 and the glory which thou gavest me I have given them; that they may be one, even as we are one:

One preacher said that one of the greatest travesties in life is that one dies without fulfilling their God-given destiny or die not finishing well.

Jesus is the way. Amen.

Chapter Nine

Gifts

1 Cor. 12:1 now concerning spiritual *gifts,* brethren, I would not have you ignorant.

1 Cor. 12:2 ye know that ye were gentiles, carried away unto these dumb idols, even as ye were led.

1 Cor. 12:3 wherefore I give you to understand, that no man speaking by the Spirit of God calleth Jesus accursed: and *that* no man can say that Jesus is the Lord, but by the Holy Ghost.

1 Cor. 12:4 now there are diversities of gifts, but the same spirit.

1 Cor. 12:5 and there are differences of administrations, but the same lord.

1 Cor. 12:6 and there are diversities of operations, but it is the same God which worketh all in all.

1 Cor. 12:7 but the manifestation of the spirit is given to every man to profit withal.

1 Cor. 12:8 for to one is given by the spirit the word of wisdom; to another the word of knowledge by the same spirit;

1 Cor. 12:9 to another faith by the same spirit; to another the gifts of healing by the same spirit;

1 Cor. 12:10 to another the working of miracles; to another prophecy; to another discerning of spirits; to another *divers* kinds of tongues; to another the interpretation of tongues:

1 Cor. 12:11 but all these worketh that one and the selfsame spirit, dividing to every man severally as he will.

1 Cor. 12:12 for as the body is one, and hath many members, and all the members of that one body, being many, are one body: so also *is* Christ.

I would like to look at some of the words in this chapter, but first let's get some understanding of the scripture. Paul is the writer and he's talking to the

Corinthian church because during that time there were idols (verse 2) and different religions, sin was rampant with temple prostitutes, and they were pagans before they were saved. Now Paul was bringing these gifts back into perspective because of all the confusion between false gifts and the gifts of the Holy Spirit. He says, "I would not have you ignorant."

I want us to look at verses 4-12 in the Amplified Version.

[4] now there are distinctive varieties *and* distributions of endowments (gifts, [a]extraordinary powers distinguishing certain Christians, due to the power of divine grace operating in their souls by the Holy Spirit) and they vary, but the [Holy] spirit remains the same.

[5] and there are distinctive varieties of service *and* ministration, but it is the same lord [who is served].

[6] and there are distinctive varieties of operation [of working to accomplish things], but it is the same God who inspires *and* energizes them all in all.

[7] but to each one is given the manifestation of the [Holy] spirit [the evidence, the spiritual illumination of the spirit] for good *and* profit.

[8] to one is given in *and* through the [Holy] spirit [the power to speak] a message of wisdom, and to another [the power to express] a word of knowledge *and* understanding according to the same [Holy] spirit;

[9] to another [[h]wonder-working] faith by the same [Holy] spirit, to another the extraordinary powers of healing by the one spirit;

[10] to another the working of miracles, to another prophetic insight ([i] the gift of interpreting the divine will and purpose); to another the ability to discern *and* distinguish between [the utterances of true] spirits [and false ones], to another various kinds of [unknown] tongues, to another the ability to interpret [such] tongues.

[11] all these [gifts, achievements, abilities] are inspired *and* brought to pass by one and the same [Holy] spirit, who apportions to each person individually [exactly] as he chooses.

[12] for just as the body is a unity and yet has many parts, and all the parts, though many, form [only] one body, so it is with Christ (the Messiah, the Anointed One).

The word that has always been in contention in the body of Christ is "gifts" because some say these all passed away with the apostles. Well I differ from that train of thought and deception, but I must say that I believe that the body is coming into unity in these areas. Ephesians talks about unity of the faith. Lord, come quickly.

One of the words I would like to look at is <u>diversities of gifts</u> in the King James Version

But if you notice in the Amplified Version, it says:

Varieties *and* distributions of endowments which mean to *separate*, that is, *distribute:*—divide. (Strong's Concordance) so Paul is dividing the gifts so as to distinguish one from another.

The next word is **diversities of operations** an *effect:*—operation, working, in the King James Version. The Amplified Version really spells it out, varieties of operation [of working to accomplish things].

The thesaurus says it is a process, actions, acts, procedures, and function.

In other words, we don't operate the same when we minister, but the scripture says it is by the same Holy Ghost. I'm not talking about being in the flesh when you minister. I had a minister with our church one time, and the glory was so powerful, I was walking around because you couldn't stand still. Someone who was thinking about joining the ministry came to me and said her husband was outside and very angry. I went outside, and he said he had a headache because one of the ministers had hit him in the head trying to get him to fall down. I had to deal with the minister, of course, but that family said they would never come back again because he was in the flesh.

While ministering to that minister, I found out he saw someone else doing that and it worked for them, so he decided to try it too.

I'm talking about when you know God's voice and the Holy Spirit is leading you to operate in a way that pleases him.

I want to reiterate something: because people have made mistakes, they don't want to try again. However, I heard someone say if you've never made a mistake, you've probably never done anything.

That minister who hit the man in the head listened to my council and sat out of ministry for a year. Now he is pastoring a church in the Midwest and is still a son in the ministry. He is doing well, praise God.

If I could sum up this chapter, it would be to say "don't be afraid to be different." God has called you in your unique way to be used with your personality. He will take what you have and anoint it for his glory.

Note: Read the verses listed in the next chapter out loud in a quiet place.

Chapter Ten

The Box of Fear

I believe that anyone can conquer fear by doing
the things he fears to do, provided he keeps doing
them until he gets a record of successful experiences
behind him.

—Eleanor Roosevelt

Never be afraid to try something new. Remember,
amateurs built the ark. Professionals built the *Titanic*.

—Unknown

One of the boxes we have erected is fear. The Bible
teaches us that God has not given us a spirit of fear,
but of power, of love, and of a sound mind. (2 Tim.
1:7)

Let's take a look at this scripture in its context,

2 Tim. 1:4 greatly desiring to see thee, being mindful of thy tears, that I may be filled with joy;

2 Tim. 1:5 when I call to remembrance the unfeigned faith that is in thee, which dwelt first in thy grandmother Lois, and thy mother Eunice; and I am persuaded that in thee also.

2 Tim. 1:6 wherefore I put thee in remembrance that thou stir up the gift of God, which is in thee by the putting on

2 Tim. 1:7 for God hath not given us the spirit of fear; but of power, and of love, and of a sound mind.

2 Tim. 1:8 be not thou therefore ashamed of the testimony of our Lord, nor of me his prisoner: but be thou partaker of the afflictions of the gospel according to the power of God;

Paul is telling Timothy that he has gifts in him that came down through his grandmother and his mother, plus Paul and possibly others had laid hands on Timothy to impart some spiritual gifts.

Why do I say this is one of the quotes that says never be afraid to try something new? We think in the box, and we put God in our little boxes that say, I can't do that because I've never had the teaching or I've never been to seminary or I've never done this or done that. You don't understand I have this difficult time doing this. The bottom line is you probably never tried so you will never succeed until you try. Amateurs built the ark, but professionals built the Titanic. I will spell it out—the ark never sunk.

The word of God always encourages us to push forward, not draw back. Hebrews 10:38-39

38 now the just shall live by faith: but if *any man* draw back, my soul shall have no pleasure in him.

39 but we are not of them who draw back unto perdition; but of them that believe to the saving of the soul.

The word perdition means *ruin* or *loss in the Greek also g575 reversal*, or danger (Strong's), we don't shrink back we move forward, advance daily with the leading of the Holy Spirit, Philippians 4:13 says we can do all things through Christ who strengthens us. We should say this to ourselves daily until it gets in our spirit and the Word comes alive in our hearts. Then we will not manifest fear and timidity

Another area we have boxes is that only certain people can do certain things. The Bible clearly states in Mark 16:17-18:

17 and these signs shall follow them that believe; in my name shall they cast out devils; they shall speak with new tongues;

18 they shall take up serpents; and if they drink any deadly thing, it shall not hurt them; they shall lay hands on the sick, and they shall recover. (KJV)

The prerequisite here is you only have to be a believer. Wow, that is the only requirement. Amazing! So now, just because you don't have a doctors degree or college education, or come from a particular denomination or religion, you can do all things through Christ.

Another quote that helped me in writing this book was by John Wayne: Courage is being scared to death—and saddling up anyway.—*John Wayne.*

2 Cor. 12:9 and he said unto me, my grace is sufficient for thee: for my strength is made perfect in weakness. Most gladly therefore will I rather glory in my infirmities, that the power of Christ may rest upon me.

2 Cor. 12:10 therefore I take pleasure in infirmities, in reproaches, in necessities, in persecutions, in distresses for Christ's sake: for when I am weak, then am I strong.

When I am weak, then am I strong because of the empowering grace of God that he has given to us. Let's receive it today and put fear away from us forever. Thusly, taking God out of the box that we have erected, which was keeping us from really being all he created us to be and do.

Eleanor Roosevelt believed that anyone can conquer fear, and I do too. If God didn't give it to you, discard it now and do the work of the Lord.

If you need help in that area, seek counsel and prayer from someone you trust: your pastor, etc.

Chapter Eleven

The Faithfulness of God

Recently the Lord told me to trust him with my pain. That takes trust in God's word and what it says about him. Have I truly trusted in him? If I haven't, then I probably don't have confidence in His faithfulness to be and do what His promises say about Him. But as we experience his love and faithfulness, this will change day by day, week by week, month by month, etc.

There are some areas of our lives that we struggle in. One is stepping into the uncomfortable places. The media and our circumstances have kept people wanting to be comfortable. In Christ we will always have to do something different so that we can grow and increase. Without this we will remain the same or just exist. But not making an impact on the world or those around us, I have several questions: Do you really want to grow? Do you want to change everything in the sphere of your influence?

Because God is faithful, you can do it. He said that you can do all things through Christ who strengthens you. (Phil. 4:13) All His promises are yes and amen.

> 2 Cor. 1:20 for all the promises of God in him *are* yea, and in him amen, unto the glory of God by us.

> Heb. 8:6 but now hath he obtained a more excellent ministry, by how much also he is the mediator of a better covenant, which was established upon better promises.

> Heb. 6:13 for when God made promise to Abraham, because he could swear by no greater, he sware by himself,

> Heb. 6:14 saying, surely blessing I will bless thee, and multiplying I will multiply thee.

> Heb. 6:15 and so, after he had patiently endured, he obtained the promise.

> Heb. 6:16 for men verily swear by the greater: and an oath for confirmation *is* to them an end of all strife.

> Heb. 6:17 wherein God, willing more abundantly to shew unto the heirs of promise

the immutability of his counsel, confirmed *it* by an oath:

Heb. 6:18 that by two immutable things, in which *it was* impossible for God to lie, we might have a strong consolation, who have fled for refuge to lay hold upon the hope set before us:

Heb. 6:19 which *hope* we have as an anchor of the soul, both sure and stedfast, and which entereth into that within the veil.

As Abraham was given these promises, he believed God, and it was counted to him as righteousness. And because Abraham was blessed, so are we. For the blessings of Abraham have come on the gentiles—those of us who are in Christ Jesus.

Verse 13 says that God swore by himself, verses 17-18 that the two immutable things, was to confirm the promises by an oath to end all strife verse 16 (*dispute, disobedience:*—contradiction)

Some more Word: Amplified Version

Psalm 31:5 into your hands I commit my spirit; you have redeemed me, o Lord, the **God** of truth and **faithful**ness.

Psalm 57:3 he will send from heaven and save me from the slanders and reproaches of him who would trample me down or swallow me up, and he will put

him to shame. Selah [pause, and calmly think of that]!
God will send forth his mercy and loving-kindness
and his truth and **faithful**ness.

Psalm 61:7 may he sit enthroned forever before [the
face of] **God**; o ordain that loving-kindness and
faithfulness may watch over him!

Psalm 69:13 but as for me, my prayer is to you, o
Lord. At an acceptable and opportune time, o **God**,
in the multitude of your mercy and the abundance of
your loving-kindness hear me, and in the truth and
faithfulness of your salvation answer me.

Psalm 71:22 I will also praise you with the harp, even
your truth and faithfulness, o my **God**; unto you will I
sing praises with the lyre, o holy one of Israel.

Psalm 78:8 and might not be as their fathers—a
stubborn and rebellious generation, a generation that
set not their hearts aright nor prepared their hearts to
know **God**, and whose spirits were not steadfast and
faithful to **God**.

Psalm 89:8 o Lord **God** of Hosts, who is a mighty one
like unto you, o Lord? And your faithfulness is round
about you [an essential part of you at all times].

Psalm 98:3 he has [earnestly] remembered his mercy
and loving-kindness, his truth and his faithfulness
toward the house of Israel; all the ends of the earth
have witnessed the salvation of our **God**.

Psalm 119:86 all your commandments are faithful and sure. [The godless] pursue and persecute me with falsehood; help me [Lord]!"

Isaiah 25:1 o Lord, you are my **God**; I will exalt you, I will praise your name, for you have done wonderful things, even purposes planned of old [and fulfilled] in faithfulness and truth.

Isaiah 65:16 so [it shall be] that he who invokes a blessing on himself in the land shall do so by saying, may the **God** of truth and fidelity [the amen] bless me; and he who takes an oath in the land shall swear by the **God** of truth and faithfulness to his promises [the amen], because the former troubles are forgotten and because they are hidden from my eyes.

If we draw nigh to God he will draw near to us (James 4:8a, KJV).

For he is faithful indeed trust him.

Philippians 4:19 but my God shall supply all your need according to his riches in glory by Christ Jesus.

I remember when the church needed a carpet real bad and we had no way to purchase the carpet. One day, my spiritual son and I were in the sanctuary and the Lord said, "Take up the carpet." We started right then in obedience and we started with the boarders and proceeded from there. As we did that, I found eleven cents in one corner, and my son found the same thing in the other corner. We stopped, and I went to the office and got my book on the Prophetic meaning of numbers and found out that eleven was incompleteness, disorder, disorganization, imperfection, lack of fulfillment, or disintegration. Read Acts 1:15-26 about the apostles. We prayed and broke off all curses and released the blessing, and two weeks later, we had a brand-new carpet for almost nothing. The owner of the carpet store installed it for nothing down. Oh yes, we prayed for him, and God healed him of severe pain in his legs. Our God is faithful and true to his word. We needed that carpet. I can write a book on the things he's done for us. Wow, to God be the glory.

Chapter Twelve

Change Your Thinking

I beseech you therefore, brethren, by the mercies of God, that ye present your bodies a living sacrifice, holy, acceptable unto God, *which is* your reasonable service. And be not conformed to this world, but be ye transformed by the renewing of your mind, that ye may prove what *is* that good, and acceptable, and perfect, will of God. Romans 12:1-2

Verse 2 uses the phrase, transformed by the renewing of your mind, and the word transformed comes from the Greek word metamorphoō

Met-am-or-fo'-o

From g3326 and g3445; to *transform* (literally or figuratively "metamorphose"):—change, transfigure, transform.

To change the way you think, this word is the same word we get metamorphosis from in the changing of a moth to a butterfly, a tadpole into a frog, etc. This change will transform you from poverty to wealth, from sickness into health, from bondage to freedom, amen.

This will only happen when we change our input. The Word of God is the proven way to change your thinking. We must read it daily so that it will become effective in our lives.

I heard a long time ago that we must eat food every day or we will get physically weak. It's the same way with your spirit. We are a spirit living in a body (2 Corinthians 5:2-4).

WATCH YOUR THOUGHTS, FOR THEY BECOME WORDS

WATCH YOUR WORDS, FOR THEY BECOME ACTIONS

WATCH YOUR ACTIONS, FOR THEY BECOME HABITS

WATCH YOUR HABITS, FOR THEY BECOME CHARACTER

WATCH YOUR CHARACTER, FOR IT BECOMES YOUR DESTINY

There have been so many things we have experienced in our lives that have influenced our thinking patterns: abuse of all kinds, social pressure, wrong relationships, and wrong input. But the good news is there's hope in Christ. Our God is a mind regulator, if we allow him to be one for us. I was always afraid of flying until, one day, I was flying to the Philippines, and the Lord said to me, "Living or dead, I have you in my hands." Wow, it so liberating. As I heard that, peace came over me, and my thinking was changed about flying and plane accidents as well as dying. One little word from the Lord changed me forever.

Something else I learned from Mother Jean about flying is when the pilot comes on the speaker and says, "Please fasten your seat belts. We will be experiencing some turbulence for a while." I just cancel that word and I say, "Peace, be still, and our God is faithful." The light goes out, and now we are free to fly without that restriction of not being able to get out of our seats.

This brings a great point to me. I can change my thinking about circumstances, and I can change the results or the way I deal with them. Philippians 4:6-8 tells us to pray about everything, think on certain things, and the peace of God will keep your hearts and minds right. And not only the peace of God, but the God of Peace himself, will be with you in every situation. Note that it's according to your thinking and actions.

The heart has a strong part of our actions and perceptions. Proverbs 23:7a says, "As he thinketh in his heart, so is he." The context of the scripture is deception. This person's heart is not in agreement with the Word. We must have discernment in these last days. Discernment speaks of wisdom, which is the principle thing. Proverbs tells us wisdom should be chosen rather than find silver or riches.

The dictionary defines wisdom like this: Wisdom is a deep understanding and realization of people, things, events or situations, resulting in the ability to apply perceptions, judgments and actions in keeping with this understanding. It often requires control of one's emotional reactions (the "<u>passions</u>") so that universal principles, reason and knowledge prevail to determine one's actions. Wisdom is also the comprehension of what is true coupled with optimum judgment as to action. Synonyms include: sagacity, discernment, or insight.

This book is about the faithfulness of God outside of the box. The box is really the way I perceive things in the way I was brought up or the way people treated me or the way I was taught, and my childhood thinking. Paul says that when he was a child, he spoke, understood, and thought as a child. But when he became a man, he put those things away (the childish things).

Hebrews 6:1 Amplified Version therefore let us go on and get past the elementary stage in the teachings *and* doctrine of Christ (the Messiah), advancing steadily toward the completeness *and* perfection that belong to spiritual maturity. Let us not again be laying the foundation of repentance *and* abandonment of dead works (dead formalism) and of the faith [by which you turned] to God.

Before we go further, let's look at the context. We must go back to chapter 5 of Hebrews, the last three verses of the King James Version (12-14):

> 12 For when for the time ye ought to be teachers, ye have need that one teach you again which *be* the first principles of the oracles of God; and are become such as have need of milk, and not of strong meat.

> 13 For every one that useth milk *is* unskilful in the word of righteousness: for he is a babe.

> 14 But strong meat belongeth to them that are of full age, *even* those who by reason of use have their senses exercised to discern both good and evil.

These scriptures are talking about maturing, going on to perfection, moving from where you are presently to the designed purpose of God for your life and ministry. We are called and chosen for a holy calling.

I remember I had a dream about eighteen years ago. In this dream, the Lord spoke to me and said that the body of Christ is anemic. At the time, I was perplexed and I said why, and he said that they have not embarrassed the fivefold ministry of the apostle, prophet, evangelist, pastor, and teacher (even though they embraced the pastor and evangelist at that time). So I asked God what was anemic. He said that my body is weak, without power. The world is looking for the real thing. The power of God. The church must embrace the fivefold giftings now. Since then, it is constantly changing, and in some arenas, the church has begun to embrace the equipping gifts.

Ephesians 4:11-15, verse 13 says, "till we all come in the unity of the faith, and of the knowledge of the Son of God, unto a perfect man, unto the measure of the stature of the fullness of Christ."

The fullness of Christ—the Anointed One, the Christ, the Son of the Living God—is coming back. Jesus is coming back for a victorious, powerful church without spot or wrinkle or anything that's less than he left. I must say it's not about signs and wonders as it is being obedient to his Word. He said, "If you love me, keep my commandments." Obedience is better than sacrifice.

The youth of today is running after God, and they are doing great things for Christ. Don't get me wrong. I believe in signs and wonders, but we must find out what Papa wants and do that. Man shall not live by bread alone but by every word that precedes from the mouth of God. That will change your way of thinking and make you known in the earth as one who has been with God.

As God gave Adam and Eve dominion over everything, so has he given us dominion. Let's walk it daily, amen.

Changed thinking brings changed results everytime.